One Day at a Time

30 Day Devotional

Ayannah Williams

Copyright © 2016 Ayannah Williams

All rights reserved. No portion of the book may be reproduced or utilized in any form or by any means, electronic or mechanical, including photocopying, recording, or by any other information storage and retrieval system, without permission in writing from the author.

TABLE OF CONTENTS

Acknowledgements 5
Day 1   "Holy Spirit" 9
Day 2   "Call on God" 13
Day 3   "Don't Lose Your Position" 17
Day 4   "Guard Your Gates" 21
Day 5   "A Solomon Blessing" 25
Day 6   "The Love of God" 29
Day 7   "Kingdom Financers" 33
Day 8   "Speak To Your Situation" 37
Day 9   "Give Thanks" 41
Day 10   "It's Only a Test" 45
Day 11   "Sow Your Way Out" 49
Day 12   "Be a Giver" 53
Day 13   "Recover All- The God of Restoration" 57
Day 14   "The Glory Zone" 61
Day 15   "Power to Overcome" 65
Day 16   "Your Faith Will Be Tested" 69
Day 17   "What Do You See?" 73
Day 18   "Your Breakthrough Draws Nigh" 77
Day 19   "Fasting Brings Victory" 81
Day 20   "You Are Seated in Heavenly Places" 85
Day 21   "You're Not Alone" 89

Day 22	"Find Your Jonathan"	93
Day 23	"Just the Way You Are"	97
Day 24	"This Battle Belongs to God"	101
Day 25	"Search Your Heart"	105
Day 26	"Something Greater"	109
Day 27	"A New Song"	113
Day 28	"It's Already in You"	117
Day 29	"A New Thing"	121
Day 30	"You Win"	125

ACKNOWLEDGEMENTS

I personally want to dedicate this book to my Lord and Savior Jesus Christ. I am more than grateful that He saved me and baptized me with the Holy Ghost.

A special thanks to my Pastor and 1st Lady, Pastor Jimmy and Alisa Wilson (East Fernwood Missionary Baptist Church), for believing in the God in me and for the many prayers. God used my Pastor twice to prophesy this book to me and now it has come to pass. Thank you both for being faithful, loving, Spirit led Leaders.

A loving thanks to my Mom, Lavannah and my Dad, Doug for being outstanding God-fearing parents who love me unconditionally. Your prayers changed my life. You both mean so much to me and I love you dearly. I thank God for you!

To my family, friends, church family and those who have encouraged me along the way, thank you for your kindness and prayers. May God bless you.

To all of those reading this book, may your life be enriched, blessed and forever changed, in the name of Jesus.

"Salvation - A Free Gift"

Scripture: "That if thou shalt confess with thy mouth the Lord Jesus, and shalt believe in thine heart that God hath raised him from the dead, thou shalt be saved. For with the heart man believeth unto righteousness; and with the mouth confession is made unto salvation."

Romans 10: 9-10

Are you Saved? If you died at this moment, are you confident that you would spend eternity with Christ? If you aren't sure, then TODAY is your day!

The most important decision you will ever make in your life is to give your life to Jesus Christ. The whole purpose of our earthly existence is to be in fellowship with God. He desires a close relationship with YOU. Jesus died so that you could live a life free from the bondage of sin and death. When you accept Jesus into your heart, you receive a new beginning, a fresh start and a brand new way of living. All you have to do is believe!

Are you ready to receive Christ now? Say this prayer out loud as your confession that you believe.

PRAYER OF SALVATION:

Dear Jesus, I believe You are the Son of God. I believe You died for me on the cross and shed Your blood for my sins. I believe that God raised You from the dead and You are now seated at the right hand of the Father. I recognize that I am a sinner and I repent of my sins. Please forgive my sins and wash me with Your blood. Come into my heart. Save my soul as I give my life to You. I make You My Lord and Savior. Fill me with Your Spirit. I will now live the rest of my life for You. I am Born Again. In the name of Jesus, Amen.

You Did It! You are Saved! The Bible declares that when one sinner repents, angels rejoice! 2 Corinthians 5:17 "Therefore if any man be in Christ, he is a new creature: old things are passed away behold all things become new." You are brand new! Welcome to the Kingdom of GOD!!!

Day 1

"Holy Spirit"

Scripture: "But the Comforter, which is the Holy Ghost, whom the Father will send in my name, he shall teach you all things, and bring all things to your remembrance, whatsoever I have said unto you."

John 14:26

Who is the Holy Spirit? He is the Spirit of God and a gift from God. Romans 8:9 declares that "if any man have not the Spirit of Christ, he is none of His". Being filled with the Holy Spirit is more important than the next breath you are about to take. The Holy Spirit is the love of your life and your only help. He is the reality of Jesus Christ. God gives us His Spirit so that we may know Him in a more intimate way and so that we may live a life that is pleasing in God's sight.

The Holy Spirit is our Advocate with the Father, our Helper, our Guide, our Friend and our Comforter. He helps us in our weaknesses and intercedes on our behalf according to the will of God with groanings which cannot be uttered. He causes the love of God to be poured into our hearts as He leads us and guides us. The Holy Spirit teaches us all things and brings all things that God has spoken to our remembrance. He declares to us the things that are to come. Once the Spirit of the Lord comes upon you, He gives you power to be God's witnesses, the anointing to preach the Gospel to the poor, power to heal the brokenhearted, authority to proclaim liberty to the captives, power to give sight to the blind and raise the dead.

Can't you see the importance of having the Holy Spirit in your life? Ask God to fill you with His precious Holy Spirit. Luke 11:13 states, "If you then, who are evil, know how to give good gifts to your children, how much more will the heavenly Father give the Holy Spirit to those who ask Him". God desires to give His Spirit to those who believe!

Prayer: Father, in the name of Jesus, I realize the significance of being filled with Your Holy Spirit. My desire is to please You in every area of my life. I cannot do this alone. I ask that You fill me with the Holy Spirit and I thank You that You've heard my prayer. In Jesus' mighty name, Amen.

Day 2

"Call on God"

Scripture: "O Lord, our Lord, how excellent is thy name in all the earth! who hast set thy glory above the heavens"

Psalm 8:1

If ever you go into prayer and you don't know what to say, just begin to call on the name of the Lord. The Bible declares, "The name of the Lord is a strong tower: the righteous runneth into it, and is safe." (Proverbs 18:10). "Seek ye the Lord while He may be found, call ye upon Him while He is near." (Isaiah 55:6). "And it shall come to pass, that before they call, I will answer; and while they are yet speaking, I will hear." (Isaiah 65:24) God understands and hears even your faintest cry. Call on Him!

LORD You are … Emmanuel, The Lion of the Tribe of Judah, a Strong Tower, the Ancient of Days, Alpha and Omega, the Beginning and the End, the First and the Last, which is and which was and which is to come, the Great I Am, Our Shepherd, Almighty, All Powerful, The Living Word, my Refuge, my Fortress, my Shield and my Buckler, Wonderful Counselor, The Lily of the Valleys, the Bright and Morning Star, The Lamb of God, the Root and the Offspring of David, a Healer, a Deliverer, a Helper, my Savior, Redeemer, Author and Finisher of our faith, the Resurrection, the Way, the Truth, the Life, Faithful and True, The Rose of Sharon, my Advocate, High Priest, the One and True Living God, Most High, Lord of Lords, King of Kings, Prince of Peace, King of Glory, Jehovah, El Shaddai, Messiah, The Anointed One, The Bread of Life, Consuming Fire, my Hiding Place, my Dwelling Place, The Vine, The Potter, The Lord of Hosts, Living Water, Our Banner… When you call on the name of the Lord, He promises to answer!

Prayer: Father, in the name of Jesus, I thank You that Your name reigns above all names. I bless Your holy name. Thank You that when I call, You hear me and You answer. May Your name be forever lifted up. In Jesus' name, Amen.

Day 3

"Don't Lose Your Position"

Scripture: *"Behold, to obey is better than sacrifice, and to hearken than the fat of rams."*

1 Samuel 15:22

God requires that we are obedient to His Word, His will and His way. Disobedience brings about punishment. Take a look at King Saul in 1 Samuel chapter 15. God gave Saul a command to destroy everything, including the people and livestock, in the city of Amalek. Saul slaughtered the people but spared Agag, the King of the Amalekites. He even kept the best of the livestock. This was not what God had commanded Saul to do. So God sent the Prophet Samuel to address Saul. Saul admitted that he had done what the people wanted him to do and disobeyed the commands of the Lord. However, instead of Saul repenting unto God first, He repented unto the Prophet Samuel (1 Samuel 15: 24-25). Granting that he disobeyed God, God stripped the Kingdom from Saul and took His anointing and presence away from Saul. Consequently, as a result, King Saul lost his position.

The Bible tells us in Lamentations 3 that the Lord's mercies are new every morning. But we must be careful that we do not continue on in sin that grace may abound. To repent means to turn away from. 1 John 1:9 declares "If we confess our sins, he is faithful and just to forgive us our sins, and to cleanse us from all unrighteousness."

Is there is anything in your life that is causing you to disobey God? Get rid of it. We must not allow the lust of the flesh, the lust of the eyes, and the pride of life to cause us to lose our position in the Kingdom. Ask God to cleanse you from all unrighteousness.

Prayer: Father, in the name of Jesus, I repent of all of my sins. I submit myself to You and ask that You would forgive me and cleanse me. Wash me with the Blood of Jesus and make me over again. I desire to please You. Amen.

Day 4

"Guard Your Gates"

Scripture: "And if thy right eye offend thee, pluck it out, and cast it from thee: for it is profitable for thee that one of thy members should perish, and not that thy whole body should be cast into hell. And if thy right hand offend thee, cut it off, and cast it from thee: for it is profitable for thee that one of thy members should perish, and not that thy whole body should be cast into hell."

Matthew 5: 29-30

It is important to guard our spiritual gates from anything that would lead to temptation and sin. We sometimes don't realize the demonic influences that this world tries to have on us. Though we are in the world, the Bible declares that we are not of this world. Christians should never conform to the standards of this world in order to fit in. Romans 12:2 states, "And be not conformed to this world: but be ye transformed by the renewing of your mind, that ye may prove what is that good, and acceptable, and perfect, will of God." Don't be a sellout.

1 Peter 2:9 "But ye are a chosen generation, a royal priesthood, an holy nation, a peculiar people; that ye should shew forth the praises of him who hath called you out of darkness into his marvellous light". God tells us in His Word to be holy for He is holy. This means that we are to take an aggressive stand against sin and be holy. "For the grace of God that bringeth salvation hath appeared to all men, teaching us that, denying ungodliness and worldly lusts, we should live soberly, righteously, and godly, in this present world". (Titus 2: 11-12)

You must guard your eye gates, ear gates and all spiritual gates from the things of this world. "And have no fellowship with the unfruitful works of darkness, but rather reprove them" Ephesians 5:11. So, be cautious about what you listen to. Be cautious about what you watch on TV and the kinds of books you read. Be alert about the conversations that you entertain and the places you go. "Be sober, be vigilant; because your adversary the devil, as a roaring lion, walketh about, seeking whom he may devour." (1 Peter 5:8) Guard your gates.

Prayer: Father, Your Word tells me to love not the things of this world. I repent unto You for the things I have exposed Your Spirit to through my acts of disobedience. Wash me again with the blood of Jesus and cleanse me from all unrighteousness. Thank You for Your forgiveness. In Jesus' name, Amen.

Day 5

"A Solomon Blessing"

Scripture: *"If my people, which are called by my name, shall humble themselves, and pray, and seek my face, and turn from their wicked ways; then will I hear from heaven, and will forgive their sin, and will heal their land."*

2 Chronicles 7:14

In 2 Samuel 12, God sent word by the Prophet Nathan that David's child would die. David fasted and cried unto the Lord to spare the child. However, when the baby died, David got up and worshipped the Lord and ate. For he said, "While the child was yet alive, I fasted and wept: for I said, who can tell whether God will be gracious to me, that the child may live?" David fasted and wept in hopes that God would spare his son. However, David's punishment for the sin he committed against Uriah, by having him killed and taking his wife Bathsheba, caused David to lose his child. Yet, God was gracious unto David in that He blessed David and Bathsheba with another son by the name of Solomon. Solomon was beloved of the Lord and later became one of the richest and wisest men to ever live.

Whenever God allows a thing to die in your life, release it and move forward because what's coming is greater than what you lost. Let dead things go so that God can bless you with your Solomon blessing. God is open to forgive you and restore you. His mercies are new every morning. The Lord gives and the Lord takes away, but He promises not to withhold any good thing from those that walk upright. Humble yourself, pray, seek His face and repent, and the God of Restoration will forgive your sin and heal your land. God wants to bless you!

Prayer: Father, in the name of Jesus, I repent of every sin in my life which has caused me to suffer lose. I thank You that You are gracious and merciful unto me and that You desire to restore me. My past mistakes no longer affect my future because my life and times are in Your hands and I am covered by Jesus' blood. In the name of Jesus, Amen.

Day 6

"The Love of God"

Scripture: "What is man, that thou art mindful of him? and the son of man, that thou visitest him?"

Psalm 8:4

Have you ever wondered why God loves you so much, or why does God even care? It is God's nature to love you for the Bible declares that God is love. Who can measure the love of God? Who can know the depths of His love for us? For He so loved the world that He gave His only begotten Son Jesus and Jesus so loved us that He sacrificed His life and shed His blood for our sins. The Apostle Paul writes in Romans 8:38-39, "For I am persuaded, that neither death, nor life, nor angels, nor principalities, nor powers, nor things present, nor things to come, nor height, nor depth, nor any other creature, shall be able to separate us from the love of God, which is in Christ Jesus our Lord." Nothing can separate us from God's love. It is impossible.

There is not one thing that can convince God to stop loving you. Nothing you've done and nothing you will ever do will cause God to stop showing His unfailing love towards you. He adores you and He loves you with an everlasting love. When He looks at you, He doesn't see your flaws, your weaknesses or your mistakes, but He sees His child, His creation. Oh how deep is the love of God for us. He is constantly thinking of us. Longing to show His great love towards us. He loves you!

Prayer: Father, thank You for Your unfailing love. You love me beyond my shortcomings and limitations. You love me past my failures and mistakes. I receive Your love in my life and I want to experience Your love in a new way each and every day. Thank You for loving me unconditionally. In the name of Jesus, Amen.

Day 7

"Kingdom Financers"

Scripture: *"For God is the one who provides seed for the farmer and then bread to eat. In the same way, he will provide and increase your resources and then produce a great harvest of generosity in you."*

2 Corinthians 9:10 (NLT)

As a minister of the Gospel, refuse to be broke. In Luke 22:35, Jesus asked the 12 apostles if they lacked anything while on their journey, and they replied, "We lacked nothing".

Reject lack of any kind, for God promises to supply all of your needs according to His riches in Glory (Philippians 4:19). Refuse to go without what you need because God declares that no good thing will He withhold from them who walk uprightly (Psalm 84:11). Stand firm against the lies of the enemy telling you that it is ok not to prosper, for God says "Beloved, I wish above all things that thou mayest prosper" (3 John 1:2). Bind that spirit of poverty and lack in your mind and in your life.

Declaration: In the name of Jesus, I rebuke every spirit that would try to keep you broke and in poverty. I speak that the wealth of the wicked is no longer stored up, but that it is being released to those who can believe and receive. I decree that there will be Kingdom Builders reading this book who will be able to finance the Kingdom of God. There will be those who can support the needs of others in the Body of Christ. There will be individuals who can write the vision and make it plain and there will be persons who can run with it. I decree and declare that as you give, it shall be given unto you. No more lack of any kind, in the mighty name of Jesus.

Refuse to be broke! Say out loud, "I refuse to be broke, in the name of Jesus."

Prayer: Father, I thank You that You desire to bless me financially to be a Kingdom Builder and a Kingdom Blesser. I release my faith as a currency in the heavens that I may receive more seed in the natural. My desire is to up build Your Kingdom. Bless me so that I may bless others. In the name of Jesus, Amen.

Day 8

"Speak To Your Situation"

Scripture: "Death and life are in the power of the tongue: and they that love it shall eat the fruit thereof."

Proverbs 18:21

The enemy hates when we speak life and victory over our situations. The devil desires to destroy us with any weapon he can use against us. But the Bible says that death and life are in the power of the tongue. What does that mean? It means that when the enemy comes to attack you, speak to him by declaring God's Word. In Matthew chapter 4, Jesus, being full of the Holy Ghost, was led by the Spirit into the wilderness to be tempted of the devil. Yet, with each attempt that Satan used, Jesus combated him with the Word of God. Hebrews 4:12 declares, "For the word of God is quick, and powerful, and sharper than any two-edged sword, piercing even to the dividing asunder of soul and spirit, and of the joints and marrow, and is a discerner of the thoughts and intents of the heart." The Word is a weapon of warfare. Use it!

Declaration: I decree and declare that…"No weapon formed against me shall prosper" (Isaiah 54:17); "I can do ALL things through Christ who strengthens me" (Philippians 4:13); "I am more than a conqueror" (Romans 8:37); "I am healed" (1 Peter 2: 24); "I am delivered" (Colossians 1:13); "I am free" (Romans 8:1); "I am fearfully and wonderfully made" (Psalm 139:14); I bind the enemy in my life (Matthew 18:18) in the mighty name of Jesus.

Call on the name of Jesus and speak to your situation. James 2:19 declares that even the devils believe in God and they fear and tremble. Speak to that spirit of worry, depression, suicide, sexual desires, sickness, homosexuality, low self-esteem, jealousy, alcoholism, drug addiction, gossiping, and discouragement and command it to leave in the name of Jesus! Speak over your life and let the devil know that he is already defeated! You DO NOT have to be controlled any longer by these spirits! Give God the praise, for He has given you the Victory!

Prayer: Father, I thank You for Your Word which has power to overthrow Satan. I follow Jesus' example by using the Word as a weapon of spiritual warfare. You have given me authority to declare victory over myself and my family. Thank You. In the name of Jesus, Amen.

Day 9

"Give Thanks"

Scripture: "Speaking to yourselves in psalms and hymns and spiritual songs, singing and making melody in your heart to the Lord; Giving thanks always for all things unto God and the Father in the name of our Lord Jesus Christ."

Ephesians 5: 19-20

Sometimes when we are going through trying situations, God desires to change us more than the situation. Meaning, He wants us to learn how to give Him praise even when things aren't looking good. The Bible says in 1 Thessalonians 5:18, "In every thing give thanks: for this is the will of God in Christ Jesus concerning you". The best way to get out of what you're going through, is to go through it. Don't let your trial be wasted.

Oftentimes we can find ourselves waiting on God to perform a specific task, yet we forget to thank Him for what He has already done. So today, just begin to thank God for everything, even the smallest things. Lord, I thank You for my family, thank You for allowing me to see this day, thank You for my health, thank You for Your Word, thank You that You let me live, thank You because when I thought about giving up, You kept me, thank You that I once was lost but now I'm found, thank You that when I was alone, You were there, thank You when I thought I wouldn't make it, Your Grace was sufficient. Lord, I just say Thank You! In EVERYTHING, remember to give thanks!

Prayer: Father, if I had 10,000 tongues, I still couldn't thank You enough for all You've done. My soul will boast in You Lord. I give praise to Your Holy name. In the name of Jesus, Amen.

Day 10

"It's Only a Test"

Scripture: *"When thou passest through the waters, I will be with thee; and through the rivers, they shall not overflow thee; when thou walkest through the fire, thou shalt not be burned; neither shall the flame kindle upon thee."*

Isaiah 43:2

The truth is, you will be tested. Whether in your finances, in your health, in your marriage, in your ministry, in your attitude or on your job, tests will come. It is necessary to prove to the enemy that the anointing you have is real. 1 Peter 1: 6-7 reads, "Wherein ye greatly rejoice, though now for a season, if need be, ye are in heaviness through manifold temptations: That the trial of your faith, being much more precious than of gold that perisheth, though it be tried with fire, might be found unto praise and honour and glory at the appearing of Jesus Christ." Rejoice that you are a partaker of Christ's sufferings and that the tests come to purify you.

When Shadrach, Meshach and Abed-nego made a stand for God, they were bound and thrown into a burning fiery furnace (Daniel 3). Yet, a fourth man in the form like the Son of God, appeared in the furnace with them, and the three Hebrew boys were neither burned, nor singed nor did they smell like fire. You can be confident that in your testing and trials, God is right there with you. He promised to never leave you nor forsake you.

The fire wasn't designed to kill you. It was designed to purge you, prove you and make you as well as others, believers that God is more than able to deliver on time.

Prayer: Father, I thank You that You are with me. I pray that my faith won't fail me in my times of testing and trials. I refuse to bow to the tactics of the enemy and I look towards the hills where my help comes from because all of my help comes from You. Father, help me. In Jesus' name, Amen.

Day 11

"Sow Your Way Out"

Scripture: "But I say this, He which soweth sparingly shall reap also sparingly; and he which soweth bountifully shall reap also bountifully."

2 Corinthians 9:6

God once spoke to me and said that there are times when you can "Praise your way out" and there are times when you can "Pray your way out", but there are also times when you can "Sow your way out". A seed sown in faith has the power to break the back poverty and lack of any kind in your life. It was after Solomon offered up a thousand burnt offerings that God appeared to him in a dream by night and had a direct, one-on-one conversation with Solomon's inner spirit man. Solomon's offering got God's attention, and though Solomon asked God for wisdom, God blessed him with great wisdom and abundant wealth.

The truth is, God wants to bless you exceeding abundantly above all you could ask or think. As God leads you, release what you have as a seed offering unto God. For He is the God who gives seed to the sower according to 2 Corinthians 9:10. The same God multiplies your seed and increases the fruits of your righteousness. We serve a God who desires to bless us beyond (exceeding) overflow (abundantly). He wants to exceed what you consider to be abundance.

Prayer: God, thank You that You desire for me to prosper. Your Word declares that You give me power to get wealth. Speak to my heart concerning the seed/seeds You desire for me to sow. I trust You with my finances and I believe that You are more than able and faithful to bring the increase. In the name of Jesus, Amen.

Day 12

"Be a Giver"

Scripture: "Then Jesus beholding him loved him, and said unto him, One thing thou lackest: go thy way, sell whatsoever thou hast, and give to the poor, and thou shalt have treasure in heaven: and come, take up the cross, and follow me."

Mark 10:21

God takes care of those who take care of others. Some of the simple joys in life come from the charities you do for people. A simple smile, a word of encouragement, a hug; all of these things are seeds God can use to enrich the lives of others. Be a giver of not only your substance and finances, but also be a giver of your love, your time, your knowledge, and the gifts that God has placed in you. Life in the Kingdom is not about what others can do for you; it's about what you can do for others. Live a selfless life, and in everything you do, do it as unto the Lord. He is the only one who can truly reward you. For great will be your reward here on earth as well as in heaven. "But when you give to the needy, do not let your left hand know what your right hand is doing, so that your giving may be in secret. Then your Father, who sees what is done in secret, will reward you." (Matthew 6: 3-4 NIV)

So today, choose to be the light in someone else's life. Give of what you have and so shall you receive. Luke 6:38 "Give, and it shall be given unto you; good measure, pressed down, and shaken together, and running over, shall men give into your bosom. For with the same measure that ye mete withal it shall be measured to you again."

Prayer: Father, I ask that You make me a giver in all that I do. Help me to give more of my love, time and substance to all that I come in contact with. Give me a heart of compassion so that I may do Your will in a way that is pleasing unto You. In the name of Jesus, Amen.

Day 13

"Recover All- The God of Restoration"

Scripture: "And I will restore to you the years that the locust hath eaten, the cankerworm, and the caterpiller, and the palmerworm, my great army which I sent among you."

Joel 2:25

Job was mentioned in the scriptures as a man that was perfect and upright, who feared the Lord and avoided evil. However, Job went through a time of testing and great trial in which he lost everything, including his children. Nevertheless, the Bible mentions that when calamity struck Job's life, he fell to the ground and worshipped God, and in the end, God restored unto Job double for all he had lost.

In I Samuel 30, David enquired of the Lord after the Amalekites had taken all that belonged unto David and his men. Verse 8 says, "David enquired of the Lord, saying, Shall I pursue after the troop? Shall I overtake them? And He answered him, Pursue: for thou shalt surely overtake them, and without fail recover all." In the midst of everything you've lost, God desires to restore you completely and add to it. Isaiah 61:7 says "For your shame ye shall have double; and for confusion they shall rejoice in their portion: therefore in their land they shall possess the double: everlasting joy shall be unto them."

1 Peter 5:10 "In his kindness God called you to share in his eternal glory by means of Christ Jesus. So after you have suffered a little while, he will restore, support, and strengthen you, and he will place you on a firm foundation."

Declaration: I speak that everything that you lost, everything that the enemy took from you, everything that died because of unbelief, I decree and declare that the God of Restoration is going to give it back to you in abundance, in the mighty name of Jesus. For the blessing of the Lord maketh rich and with it, He adds no sorrow. Surely, you shall recover all!

Prayer: Father, thank You that You are a God of Restoration. I thank You that no good thing will You withhold from those who walk uprightly. I pray and ask for restoration in all areas of my life where I have experienced loss. You came that I might have life and life more abundantly. In the name of Jesus, Amen.

Day 14

"The Glory Zone"

Scripture: "*And if children, then heirs; heirs of God, and joint-heirs with Christ; if so be that we suffer with him, that we may be also glorified together.*"

Romans 8:17

I am sure that in almost every Christian's life, we've told God, "Lord, I want You to get the glory out of my life." I, as well as others, have learned that in order for God to get true glory out of your life, there must be continual purging. There has to be the cutting away of some things and people. John 15: 1-2 Jesus declares, "I am the true vine, and my Father is the husbandman. Every branch in me that beareth not fruit he taketh away: and every branch that beareth fruit, he purgeth it, that it may bring forth more fruit."

The truth is, the glory is found in your "suffering". Suffering crushes your will and your fleshly desires. Jesus made a powerful and dynamic statement when He said, "Father, if thou be willing, remove this cup from me: nevertheless, not my will but thine be done." (Luke 22:42)

The glory is found in your "separation". Everyone can't go where God is taking you. Separation also gives you an opportunity to grow closer to God in a more intimate way. "Come out from among them and be ye separate, says the Lord." (2 Corinthians 6:17)

The glory is found in your "secret place". That's the place where it's just you and God alone. "But thou, when thou prayest, enter into thy closet, and when thou hast shut the door, pray to the Father which is in secret; and thy Father, which seeth in secret shall reward thee openly." (Matthew 6:6)

Stay in God. Stay in His will and you'll stay in the Glory Zone.

Prayer: Father, in the name of Jesus, I desire that You get total glory out of my life. Purge my life of anything that is displeasing in Your sight. I humbly submit myself to Your Will and Your Way. Bring forth much fruit in my life. In the name of Jesus, Amen.

Day 15

"Power to Overcome"

Scripture: "And they overcame him by the blood of the Lamb, and by the word of their testimony; and they loved not their lives unto the death"

Revelation 12:11

The name "Jesus" alone is so powerful. The Bible declares in James 2:19 that demons fear and tremble at that name. When you combine the name of Jesus with the blood of Jesus, you have dynamic (dunamis) power! This means that there is no addiction, no soul tie, no temptation, no struggle or hang up that you have that Jesus can't deliver you from. The Bible states that Jesus came that He might destroy the works of the devil. In addition, when Jesus was resurrected from the dead, He rose with ALL power in His hands. Philippians 2:10 says that at the name of Jesus, every knee should bow and every tongue confess that Jesus Christ is Lord. Meaning, He's Lord over everything, including the demons. You have been given power through His blood, through His name and through your testimony to overcome.

Declaration: In the mighty name of Jesus, I decree and declare that every force working against you, your family, your ministry, your health, your life and your walk with Christ has to back up. By the power and authority given to me through Christ Jesus, I command every demonic spirit to loose its hold and leave now in Jesus' name. I bind every devil, every witch and warlock, every satanic spell and curse in the name of Jesus. I plead the blood of Jesus against it and I sever its ties in Jesus' name. I decree and declare victory in your life through the shed blood of Jesus Christ. It is so. Amen.

Prayer: Father, I thank You for the power given to me through the name and blood of Jesus Christ. For You have given me power to tread on serpents and scorpions and over all the power of the enemy and nothing by any means shall harm me. I declare that I am more than a conqueror through Christ Jesus. In Jesus' name, Amen.

Day 16

"Your Faith Will Be Tested"

Scripture: "*Consider it pure joy, my brothers and sisters, whenever you face trials of many kinds, because you know that the testing of your faith produces perseverance. Let perseverance finish its work so that you may be mature and complete, not lacking anything.*"

James 1: 2-4 (NIV)

God raised Moses up so that he would be a deliverer for the Children of Israel. As the Children of Israel grew so powerfully in number, this frightened the Egyptians. Consequently, in order to contain them, the Egyptians put the Children of Israel in bondage. This was all a part of God's divine plan. The irony of this situation is that God told Moses to go tell Pharaoh to let my people go and that the Children of Israel would be delivered, but God never told Moses that he would have to go back to Pharaoh numerous times and be rejected before the Children of Israel would be released. This is because when God speaks a thing, He speaks it as it shall be in the "end". This taught Moses to have faith and trust in God despite the fact that Pharaoh refused to let the Children of Israel go as God had spoken. However, in the end, God proved Himself so strong and mighty that Pharaoh literally forced the Children of Israel to leave.

There will be times in your Christian walk that God speaks the end of a thing but never tells you what you will have to experience before you get there. Joseph had a similar experience where God showed him in two dreams that he would be in authority, but God never showed him the rejection and the pit experience he would face along the way. However, Joseph remained faithful to God and God brought the dreams to pass. God may not let you in on all the details, but be confident in the fact that He is not a man that He should lie. Whatever He has promised you, He is faithful to perform it. Trust God!

Prayer: Father, thank You for being faithful even when I am not faithful. I thank You that Your Word shall not return unto You void, but it shall accomplish that which it was sent to do. Strengthen my faith so that it won't fail in hard times of testing. I trust You Lord. In Jesus' name, Amen.

Day 17

"What Do You See?"

Scripture: "And the Lord answered me, and said, Write the vision, and make it plain upon tables, that he may run that readeth it. For the vision is yet for an appointed time, but at the end it shall speak, and not lie: though it tarry, wait for it; because it will surely come, it will not tarry."

Habakkuk 2: 2-3

Has God ever shown you something that was so big and so amazing? Write it down. Do you have Godly desires in your heart and goals in your mind that you want to achieve? Write it down. In your prophetic dreams and visions, do you see yourself doing great things? Write it down.

Writing is a testament unto God that you trust Him and the plans that He has for your life. Writing the vision also gives God an opportunity to show Himself mighty and able to perform great works and miracles in your life. What you write (the vision), will become what you see (in reality). This is the reason we walk by faith (the vision) and not by what we currently see in our natural state. For the vision is for an appointed time. Trust God to bring the vision to pass as your prepare yourself through prayer, fasting and planning.

Prayer: Heavenly Father, thank You that my steps are ordered by You. Thank You for showing me the vision which is for an appointed time. Grant me the grace to prepare for it as I patiently wait on You to bring it to pass. In the name of Jesus, Amen.

Day 18

"Your Breakthrough Draws Nigh"

Scripture: "And when he went forth to land, there met him out of the city a certain man, which had devils long time, and ware no clothes, neither abode in any house, but in the tombs. When he saw Jesus, he cried out, and fell down before him, and with a loud voice said, What have I to do with thee, Jesus, thou Son of God most high? I beseech thee, torment me not."

Luke 8: 27-28

There was a man in the country of the Gadarenes who was possessed by a legion of demons. Jesus was on a ship headed towards that part of the country where the man was, but before Jesus arrived, a great storm arose. This storm is a representation of the hindrances, blockages, hardships and trials that arise in our lives right before we receive our breakthrough. The storm came to hinder Jesus from getting to the other side where the man with legion was because the enemy understood that great deliverance was about to take place. Satan knew that a man who was possessed by a legion of demons was about to become an Evangelist, a worshipper and a voice for Jesus. After Jesus delivered the man from the demons, He told him to return to his own house and show what great things the LORD had done for him. In Luke 8:39, the Bible exclaims, "And he went his way and published throughout the whole city how great things Jesus had done unto him." What a testimony!

Could it be that the storm you're facing right now is an indication that your breakthrough is near? Right before you give up, right before you throw in the towel, just wait on God a little while longer because your deliverance draws nigh. God is about to break every chain and destroy every yoke the enemy is using to keep you bound. When you come out, you will have a powerful testimony. In the name of Jesus, be delivered, be healed and be set free. Receive your breakthrough now!

Prayer: In the name of Jesus, I bind and paralyze every demon sent to hinder the plans and purposes of God in my life. Every act of spiritual wickedness in high places be brought down in the mighty name of Jesus. Amen.

Day 19

"Fasting Brings Victory"

Scripture: "*Then all the children of Israel, and all the people, went up, and came unto the house of God, and wept, and sat there before the Lord, and fasted that day until even, and offered burnt offerings and peace offerings before the Lord.*"

Judges 20:26

In Judges *Chapter* 20, The Children of Israel went up in battle against the Children of Benjamin. During the 1st battle, the Children of Israel were severely defeated and lost 22,000 men in battle. They enquired of the Lord whether to return to battle again or not, and the Lord directed them to "Go". In the 2nd battle, the Children of Israel lost another 18,000 men and became extremely discouraged. It was then that the Children of Israel went up to the house of God and wept before the Lord, fasted and offered burnt offerings and peace offerings. This time God spoke and encouraged the Children of Israel to go into battle once more, for this time He was going to deliver their enemies into their hands.

The irony of this biblical account is that before each battle, God spoke to the Children of Israel to "pursue". But it was not until the Children of Israel fasted before the Lord that they received the victory over their enemies. After fasting, the Children of Israel slew over 25,000 warriors from the Benjamin tribe.

Fasting unlocks victory. When you fast, you bring your will and your flesh under subjection. What you don't feed will die. It crucifies your desires and fleshly wants. The strongholds come down when you come down. Your enemies are brought down when you fast. It allows God to come on the scene with answers, revelation, power and deliverance.

Is there something in your life that you are struggling with? Is there an answer that you need from God? Is there a weakness in your life or an area that needs improvement? Seek God with prayer and fasting. Fasting gets God's attention and brings about an open reward. "But thou, when thou fastest, anoint thine head, and wash thy face; That thou appear not unto men to fast, but unto thy Father which is in secret: and thy Father, which seeth in secret, shall reward thee openly." (Matthew 6: 17-18)

Prayer: Father, in the name of Jesus, I thank You that I have victory through Christ Jesus. I realize my need for more of You in my life and I ask and pray that You would bring answers, revelation and victory in my life. I submit myself to fasting, praying and seeking You while You can be found. In Jesus' name, Amen.

DAY 20

"YOU ARE SEATED IN HEAVENLY PLACES"

Scripture: "But God, who is rich in mercy, for his great love wherewith he loved us, even when we were dead in sins, hath quickened us together with Christ, (by grace ye are saved;) and hath raised us up together, and made us sit together in heavenly places in Christ Jesus:"

Ephesians 2: 4-6

The Bible tells us in 2 Timothy 2:3 "Thou therefore endure hardness, as a good soldier of Jesus Christ." As an ambassador for Christ, there will be many battles you have to face. But be encouraged, for the enemy that you've been fighting is beneath you; the lies that have been spoken against you are beneath you; the persecution that you've suffered is beneath you. You're seated in heavenly places in Christ Jesus. This means that you war from a different realm and dimension. For the weapons of our warfare are not carnal, but mighty through God to the pulling down of strongholds (2 Corinthians 10:4). For we wrestle not against flesh and blood but against principalities, against powers, against the rulers of the darkness of this world, against spiritual wickedness in high places (Ephesians 6:12). Wherefore take unto you the whole armour of God, that ye may be able to withstand in the evil day, and having done all, to stand (Ephesians 6:13). Behold, I give unto you power to tread on serpents and scorpions, and over all the power of the enemy and nothing shall by any means hurt you (Luke 10:19).

Prayer: Father, in the name of Jesus, thank You that You have given me dominion over the enemy. But I rejoice not that the spirits are subject unto me, but rather I rejoice because my name is written in heaven. I thank You for seating me in heavenly places in Christ Jesus. Amen.

Day 21

"You're Not Alone"

Scripture: "Where can I go from your Spirit? Where can I flee from your presence? If I go up to the heavens, you are there; if I make my bed in the depths, you are there. If I rise on the wings of the dawn, if I settle on the far side of the sea, even there your hand will guide me, your right hand will hold me fast."

Psalm 139: 7-10

Oftentimes when we are going through situations and trying times in our lives, the enemy has the tendency to bring in a spirit of heaviness causing you to feel alone, dejected, rejected and even depressed, but know that you are not alone. For we wrestle not against flesh and blood, but against principalities, against powers, against the rulers of the darkness of this world, against spiritual wickedness in high places. Yet in your battle against the enemy, God promises to be with you (Isaiah 43:2). No matter how alone you may feel, you are not alone. God is right there with you. He cares so much about you and the things that are going on in your life. For we do not have a High Priest which cannot be touched with the feeling of our infirmities, but was in all points tempted like as we are, yet without sin (Hebrews 4:15). Jesus understands our feelings, our burdens and our weaknesses, yet He gives you a way out by saying "cast your cares upon Me, for I care for you" (1 Peter 5:7). When you cast your cares upon Jesus and take upon His yoke and learn of Him, He promises that you shall find rest for your soul. (Matthew 11:29)

Prayer: Heavenly Father, forgive me if I have ever treated You as if You were not there. You are faithful and true. You won't leave and You won't give up on me. Thank You for being a burden lifter. In the name of Jesus, Amen.

Day 22

"Find Your Jonathan"

Scripture: "A friend loveth at all times, and a brother is born for adversity"

Proverbs 17:17

David, a young shepherd boy, was anointed to be the next king of Israel at an early age. Though he would not take the throne immediately at that time, God began to prepare David for where he was headed. God used a divine connection with Jonathan, King Saul's son, to help train David for a Kingdom lifestyle. Jonathan instantly connected to David as the Bible states that the soul of Jonathan was knit with the soul of David and Jonathan loved him as his own soul. Jonathan's purpose in David's life was to teach David the order of the Kingdom and to push him into his divine destiny. Though it was Kingdom custom for a King's son to succeed in line to be King, Jonathan understood that David had been anointed by God to be the next King. Thus, he never let jealousy interfere with his friendship and loyalty towards David.

In order to fulfill your divine destiny, it is important to have the right people in your life. Surround yourself with people that are able to push you into the place that God is taking you. Be amongst people who are smarter than you, more anointed than you, wiser than you and people who are not jealous of you or intimidated by you. When the wrong people are in your life, wrong things happen. However, when the right people are in your life, right things happen. GOD things happen! Dreams are fulfilled; destinies are reached. Ask God to place the right people in your life and remove anyone sent with an assignment to destroy you.

Prayer: Heavenly Father, I believe the plans You have for me are of good and not evil. Divinely connect me to the people needed in this season to help push me into my destiny. I frustrate and annihilate the plans of the enemy with the blood of Jesus and ask that You would remove anything or anyone who has a diabolical assignment to distract me and destroy me. In the name of Jesus, Amen.

Day 23

"Just the Way You Are"

Scripture: "I will praise thee; for I am fearfully and wonderfully made: marvellous are thy works; and that my soul knoweth right well."

Psalm 139:14

Have you ever took a deep look at yourself on the inside and outside and all you could see were your flaws and insecurities? Despite your good, it seemed that your bad outweighed. When you view yourself negatively, you miss the authenticity of how God designed you. Psalm 139:14 declares that you are fearfully and wonderfully made. Hand crafted and designed by the Creator Himself. You are created in the image of God, unique and gifted, set apart and peculiar. Your life is important. Your testimony is needed. There is no one else like you who has the gifts that you have. Your personality is special. Your characteristics are rare. You are in fact one-of-a-kind, exceptional and extraordinary. You're a child of the Most High God; made a little lower than the angels but crowned with glory and honor. See yourself the way that God sees you. You are an achiever and an overcomer, anointed and appointed, a gift to your surroundings; a blessing to your family; an asset to the Kingdom of God. Be humble, yet confident in how God created you.

Prayer: Father, forgive me for not appreciating Your design for my life. Help me not to be critical of myself in a way that overrides Your view of me. Give me the right perception so that I can see myself the way that You see me. Show me who You have made me to be in You. I thank You that I am crowned with glory and honor. In Jesus' name, Amen.

Day 24

"This Battle Belongs to God"

Scripture: "Say to them that are of a fearful heart, Be strong, fear not: behold, your God will come with vengeance, even God with a recompence; he will come and save you."

Isaiah 35:4

There are some situations you will be put in to try you, to see how you will respond. Then there will be some situations where the enemy rises up against you because of the anointing on your life and the threat that you are to Satan. But be not afraid or dismayed. Stand still and see the salvation of the Lord. This battle belongs to God. He is going to fight for you.

In 2 Chronicles 20, there arose a great army against Jehoshaphat and all Judah and the inhabitants of Jerusalem. And Jehoshaphat feared what was to happen, but he set himself before the Lord and proclaimed a fast throughout all Judah. In the midst of seeking God for help, God spoke and said "Ye shall not need to fight in this battle; set yourselves, stand ye still and see the salvation of the Lord with you, O Judah and Jerusalem: fear not, nor be dismayed; to morrow go out against them; for the Lord will be with you" (verse 17). And they worshipped God. And when they arose the next morning, praisers were appointed to go before the army. And as they praised and sang before the Lord, God Himself set ambush against their enemies and caused the enemies to turn on one another. It took Jehoshaphat and his people three days to collect all of the spoils, riches and jewels from their enemies.

God is not asking you to fight. He's not asking you to address the lies or the persecution that you face. He's asking you to stand. Stand on His Word. Stand on His promises. Stand on the fact that vengeance belongs to Him and He shall repay.

Declaration: I decree and declare that when you stand, God is going to allow you to come out with more than you had before, in Jesus' name.

Now let God take care of it.

Prayer: Father, thank You that the fight is fixed and the battle is already won. I rejoice in the victories You have already given me. I forgive my enemies and I release the situation unto You. I do not have to fight. I have the victory, in Jesus' name, Amen.

Day 25

"Search Your Heart"

Scripture: "For if ye forgive men their trespasses, your heavenly Father will also forgive you: But if ye forgive not men their trespasses, neither will your Father forgive your trespasses."

Matthew 6: 14-15

At some point in our lives, we have all been hurt by someone close to us. A friend may have betrayed you, a spouse spoke harshly to you, a co-worker offended you or a stranger may have taken something from you. Whatever the case may be, we are commanded by God to forgive. Let it go. Even if that person never apologizes to you, you must forgive. When you forgive someone who doesn't deserve forgiveness, you are acting just as Jesus does when He forgives us for the wrongs we commit. In order to receive God's forgiveness, we must forgive others. Unforgiveness locks up your heart and restricts the hand of God in your life. In the scriptures, Jesus makes it plain that our forgiveness towards others has to be immeasurable. Take a look at the questions Peter asked Jesus. "Then Peter came to him and asked, "Lord, how often should I forgive someone who sins against me? Seven times?", "No, not seven times," Jesus replied, "but seventy times seven!" (Matthew 18: 21-22 NLT)

Today, search your heart. Is there anyone you need to forgive? Do you need to forgive yourself? Have you truly forgiven others like you should? When you forgive, God will forgive you, heal you and heal the situation.

Prayer: Heavenly Father, I thank You that Your Spirit reveals all truth. Show me anyone I need to forgive and give me the grace to forgive now. You have commanded me to forgive so that I may be forgiven. I release every hurt, every grudge, every negative word spoken and every bad memory and I ask that You heal me completely. In the name of Jesus, Amen.

Day 26

"Something Greater"

Scripture: "For I know the thoughts that I think toward you, saith the Lord, thoughts of peace, and not of evil, to give you an expected end."

Jeremiah 29:11

Saul, the son of Kish, was sent out one day to go look for his father's donkeys that had gotten lost. So Saul and his servant traveled many places looking for the donkeys, but did not find them. The servant suggested that they go find the man of God, Samuel, who could tell them where to go next to find the donkeys. However, God had something greater in mind. While Saul was looking for the donkeys, God was divinely setting him up to run into his destiny. Just a day before, God had already told the Prophet Samuel that Saul was coming and to anoint him to be the next King of Israel.

Saul had no idea that he would be chosen and anointed to be the next king. He doubted himself because he came from the smallest tribe (Tribe of Benjamin) and the least of all families in that tribe, but God had a greater plan.

Moses had a speech impediment, but he would one day lead the children of Israel out of Egypt and out of bondage. Joseph was just a dreamer; however, God had plans to make him a ruler in Egypt. David was in the field tending to sheep, nevertheless God had chosen him to be king. Saul persecuted the Saints, yet God changed his name to Paul and he became one of the greatest apostles to ever live. Rahab was a harlot, but her obedience to the will of God caused her and her family to be spared from destruction.

No matter where you come from and no matter how insignificant you think you are, God has something greater in mind for you!

Prayer: Heavenly Father, thank You for the perfect plan that You have for my life. My steps are ordered by You to bring me into my divine destiny. Remove all hindrances, stumbling blocks and insecurities as You take me into the place You have designed for me. In Jesus' name, Amen.

Day 27

"A New Song"

Scripture: "I waited patiently for the Lord; and he inclined unto me, and heard my cry. He brought me up also out of an horrible pit, out of the miry clay, and set my feet upon a rock, and established my goings. And he hath put a new song in my mouth, even praise unto our God: many shall see it, and fear, and shall trust in the Lord."

Psalm 40: 1-3

In this passage of scripture, David tells of how he waited patiently on the LORD in the midst of his pit experience. GOD heard David's cry, delivered him and put him on a new path. David declares that because of his deliverance, he was given a new song; A song of praise, worship and glory to God: a God who is able to hear your cry and set you free. David proclaims that his new praise was going to be evident to people so much so that they would begin to fear and trust in the Lord.

Think back to a time when you needed God's great deliverance. A time when it seemed as though you would never be free or happy. Now, reflect on how God heard your cry and delivered you. Think of how He changed you and restored you and how He fixed the situation and caused all things to work together for your good. Keep in mind the times you prayed and He immediately answered. How can we not sing a new song to a God who is so faithful? Because of this great God that we serve, we cannot be silent. Let praises continually be in your mouth. Let others know what God has done for you. Psalm 30:11-12 "Thou hast turned for me my mourning into dancing: thou hast put off my sackcloth, and girded me with gladness; To the end that my glory may sing praise to thee, and not be silent. O LORD my God, I will give thanks unto thee for ever." Your praise has the power to cause others to trust in the LORD!

Prayer: Father, thank You for hearing my cry and setting me free. I bless Your Holy name. You are mighty to deliver. Your songs and praises shall always be in my mouth. I give You glory for the wonderful things You have done for me. Thank You Master. In the name of Jesus, Amen.

Day 28

"It's Already in You"

Scripture: "*A man's gift maketh room for him and bringeth him before great men.*"

Proverbs 18:16

When you were born, you had every organ needed to live and grow as a human being. The same thing happened when you were Born Again. The moment that Christ came into your heart, you received everything that you needed to live a saved, successful and prosperous life. 2 Peter 1:3 says, "According as His divine power hath given unto us all things that pertain unto life and godliness." Every gift, every talent, every song, every book, every business idea, every ministry; it's already in you! God has already given you everything you need to be successful. Obedience and righteous living will cause you to experience the favor of God like never before. Psalm 1:3 promises that whatever you do shall prosper.

Prayer: Father, I thank You that You desire to prosper me. I am honored that You have given me talents, gifts and ideas. I ask for wisdom and guidance as I pursue my dreams and goals. In Jesus' name, Amen.

DAY 29

"A New Thing"

Scripture: "Remember ye not the former things, neither consider the things of old. Behold, I will do a new thing; now it shall spring forth; shall ye not know it? I will even make a way in the wilderness, and rivers in the desert."

Isaiah 43: 18-19

Have you ever felt an excitement in your spirit that something good was about to happen? You didn't quite know what it was, but you knew it was something. The truth is, God is getting ready to do a new thing in your life! The thing that's coming is far greater than you can imagine. 1 Corinthians 2:9 declares that eye hath not seen, nor ear heard, neither have entered into the heart of man, the things which God hath prepared for them that love Him. The thing that God is about to do, you haven't even heard about it! You have never imagined this in your mind. The dreams and visions that you have had, even the prophecies spoken about it are only a small portion of the big plan that God has for you! The best part about it is that not only will it bless your life, but your family and those connected to you will be blessed as well! So forget about the past. Forget about what didn't work and what didn't go right. For God says, "Behold, I am doing something brand new!" Get excited!

Prayer: Father, in the name of Jesus, I praise Your Holy name. Your love for me is unfailing and Your plans for me are excellent. Let Your perfect will be done in my life. I thank You for the new thing getting ready to happen in my life! I wait in expectancy! Amen.

Day 30

"You Win"

Scripture: "But thanks be to God, which giveth us the victory through our Lord Jesus Christ."

1 Corinthians 15:57

How awesome it is to know that we have victory through Christ Jesus. Death couldn't kill Him and the grave couldn't hold Him. And that same resurrecting power that raised Jesus from the dead now lives in us. Jesus came that He might destroy the works of the devil. That means that as a child of God, you have been given countless victories. In other words, You Win!

Declaration: In the name of Jesus, I decree and declare over your life that you are a winner! You win over poverty. You win over sickness. You win over perversion. You win over lust. You win over jealousy. You win over anger. You win over low self-esteem. You win over depression. You win over anxiety. You win over sadness. You win over grief. You win over cancer. You win over demons. You win over strongholds. You win over failure. You win over wrong thinking. You have the mind of Christ. You've got the victory. You have power. You have love. You have a sound mind. For Jesus has given you power over all the power of the enemy.

Now stand and take your rightful place in the LORD. You are more than a conqueror through Him that loved you (Romans 8:37). You shall not be defeated, in the name of Jesus. Because of the anointing on your life, what was sent to destroy you will now have to bow down and obey the Spirit of God in you. You win!

Prayer: Lord, because of You, I am victorious in every area of my life. What was sent to devastate me has been turned around for my good. In the name of Jesus, I decree victory and freedom from all of my afflictions. You promised to deliver me out of them all. In Jesus' name, Amen.